For Olivia,

the sweetest smile

of the family

Written by

Eden Molineux

Illustrated by

Nathalie Beauvois

My name is Macey.

I like riding my bike,

playing with my dog,

and putting on shows

for my mom and dad.

Sometimes,

I have trouble with my speech.

When I talk,

it can be hard for me

to say sounds and words.

This makes it tricky for people

to understand me.

It can be tough
when others don't understand
what I'm trying to say.
I feel frustrated when I can't tell
my teacher the things I know.

I feel sad

when my friends play

without me.

I want to hide

when some kids

laugh.

It helps me

when people give me time

to say what I want to say.

When they look in my eyes,

I know they are listening.

It feels good

when others pay attention

to what my words mean

and not how I say them.

I am working

on my sounds and words.

My speech pathologist

helps me at school,

and my family

practices with me

every night.

I am trying really hard,
and my speech keeps
getting better.

That's a good thing,

because I have a lot

to say!

www.ingramcontent.com/pod-product-compliance
Lightning Source LLC
Chambersburg PA
CBHW041127300426
44113CB00002B/85